Why did World War Two happen?

In 1933 Adolf Hitler became the leader of German_ quickly began to build up the German army and _n ____ started to seize land from other countries. In early 1939, Germany invaded a country called Czechoslovakia (which is now the Czech Republic and Slovakia). Britain and France warned Germany that any further invasions would be opposed. On 1 September 1939, Germany invaded Poland. Two days later, Britain and France declared war on Germany.

Think About It!

Children in danger

Imagine leaving your home, family and friends forever. Even before the war started, people in Europe were fearful. Adolf Hitler's government didn't like Jewish people. It had plans to send thousands of Jews to **concentration camps** to die. Many Jewish children were sent to Britain as **refugees** to escape these camps.

Refugee children arriving in England from Germany.

Night-time Terror

Imagine you are a child living in a town during World War Two. You've woken up to the noise of **air raid** sirens blaring. In the distance is the sound of the planes from the *Luftwaffe*, the German air force, on an air raid. Their deadly cargo of bombs might fall anywhere. It is frightening – time to head to an underground shelter for safety! Some families had homemade shelters in their gardens. Other families spent the night in public shelters, such as London tube stations.

UNDERGROUND

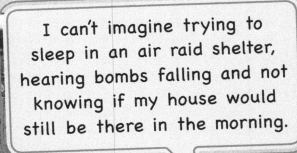

I can't imagine trying to sleep in an air raid shelter, hearing bombs falling and not knowing if my house would still be there in the morning.

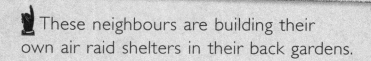

These neighbours are building their own air raid shelters in their back gardens.

4

Blitz!

The bombing of London and other cities was called the **Blitz**. Starting on 7 September 1940, London was bombed for 57 nights in a row. The Blitz continued until 21 May 1941.

Sunday 30 September 1940

In the shelter - again. Baby Alan asleep - despite racket. Marjory grizzling as usual. Mum's cuddling her. Am I scared? Yes. Am I crying? Of course not. I am almost 11 after all.

Old Mrs Hopkins in shelter with us ... Every time we hear a bomb explode she says "Cor! That was close! Do you think that one hit Albion Street?"

I try not to think about it.

Sheltering from the Blitz in a London tube station.

You Gotta Get Up in the Morning!

Imagine if you had to go outside to go to the toilet! During World War Two, many children lived in houses that had outside toilets. Brrr! Many homes had no bathroom either, so people washed in the kitchen and had baths in front of the fire. Soap and water were in short supply, so they were **rationed** by the Government. The fat and oil usually used to make soap were used for food instead. Water was rationed to one bath per person, per week.

Some children had to visit mobile bath units to have a wash.

LIFEBUOY EMERGENCY SERVICE.

HOT BATHS.

Gas masks

Could you remember to carry your smelly gas mask with you everywhere you went? At the beginning of the war, the government was afraid the Germans would attack Britain with poisonous gas. Everyone, including children, was issued with a rubber gas mask that was designed to stop them breathing in poisonous gas.

When the alarm was given, everyone had to put on their gas masks. 👉

Monday 1 October 1940

After the **all clear** sounded, went back indoors to bed. Woken up by Mum shaking me and singing at the top of her voice (which is very loud): "You gotta get up! You gotta get up in the morning!" I hate that song. It's from a film we saw about American soldiers.

Got up, pegged Alan's nappies on the line, splashed cold water round Marjory's face - she didn't half yell. Then I grabbed our gas masks from the sideboard and dragged her off to school.

The Walk to School

How do you get to school? Do you walk? During World War Two, few families had cars. Not only that, but petrol was rationed, so children had to walk to school.

Fined for wasting

For wasting petrol by leaving a lorry engine running for two minutes, Thomas Waters was yesterday fined five shillings (25p).

Daily Express, 18 October 1941

If petrol was rationed today I'd have to walk to school and that would take a long time – I'd have to get up really early!

USE SHANKS' PONY

WALK
when you can

AND EASE THE BURDEN WHICH WAR PUTS ON TRANSPORT

☛ **Government propaganda** posters, like this one, encouraged people to walk.

Bombed out

Imagine if you were walking to school on the morning after an air raid. You wouldn't know what you might find. Whole streets might have been 'bombed out'. The **Civil Defence** services might still be dealing with damage done the night before.

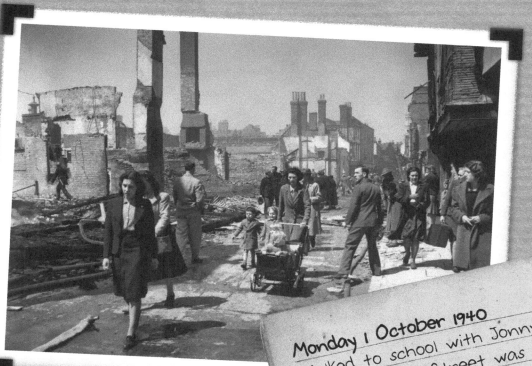

People out on the street the morning after an air raid in Canterbury, Kent.

Monday 1 October 1940
Walked to school with Jonny Wilkins. Albion Street was horrible! Some of the houses are gone completely. The rescue workers were listening for cries for help from people still trapped under the rubble.

9

Imagine arriving at school and finding it wasn't there any more! During the war, many schools were destroyed by bombing. In London, one in every five schools was hit. Teachers took classes wherever they could find a room: in churches, halls – even in pubs!

Underground classrooms

As there was a risk of a daytime air raid, schools had their own underground air raid shelters. You didn't miss lessons, though. You took your books with you down to the shelter.

Lessons continued, even when bombs were falling.

DID YOU KNOW?

Schools sometimes kept percussion instruments in the air raid shelters. Making a noise and singing helped drown out the sound of the bombing above.

Sent away for safety

At the beginning of the war, some children from towns and cities were sent away to the country, out of the way of the bombing. They were called evacuees, or 'vackees' for short. Some evacuees went to stay with relatives, but most found themselves living with total strangers.

Trains and buses took children from towns and cities to the safety of the countryside.

In the early months of the war there wasn't much bombing, so most evacuees returned home. Unfortunately, for those who lived in London and other major cities, this was just in time for the Blitz.

DID YOU KNOW?

In the country, schools became crowded with evacuees. If the weather was fine, children often had their lessons outside in a field.

Dinnertime!

Do you have school dinners, or do you take a packed lunch? Before the war, not many schools provided dinners – but, by the end of the war, one in every three children ate a school dinner. Most schools grew their own vegetables in their gardens. At break time, everyone had a small bottle of milk.

Children having their school lunch in 1942.

Wednesday 13 November 1940

Sheila, Pam and I were skipping at lunchtime. We all stopped to watch Billy Atkins arguing with Jonny.

Billy: Jonny Wilkins, you've just nicked my best marble.

Jonny: No I haven't.

Billy: Yes you have. It was a 'twelve-er'!

Billy shoved Jonny. Jonny shoved Billy back. Billy thumped Jonny. Jonny thumped Billy back. Miss Bagthorpe appeared. Marched them off to her office. Gave them both the cane. Serves them right.

Playtime

Which games do you play at break and lunchtime?
During the war, games like skipping with a rope
were popular. In the autumn, children liked
collecting conkers.

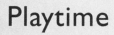 This photo, taken in
1942, shows children in
their school playground
playing with wooden hoops.

PLAYGROUND SONGS

During the war, playground songs
were very popular. Sometimes
children skipped in time to them.
Some of these songs made fun of
Hitler. One of them went:

In 1942,
old Hitler felt quite blue:
He left his pants
in the middle of France,
in 1942!

13

Afternoon Lessons

During World War Two, children had some strange lessons. Why do you think they had to learn how to mend holes in their socks, or knit scarves and woollen hats? Because factories were ordered to help the war effort by making parachutes and uniforms, **civilian** clothes were rationed. The government encouraged mothers and children to 'make do and mend', so children needed to learn new skills.

Boys learning how to darn their socks at school.

Imagine spending all afternoon at school trying to darn your socks!

Growing your own food

Food was scarce in the war, so most schools in towns started gardens or allotments where the school children worked. If you were at school in the country, you might be taken on a lorry to a farm and spend all day digging up potatoes.

To encourage children to grow and eat vegetables, the government created two cartoon characters called Dr Carrot and Potato Pete.

DOCTOR CARROT
the Children's best friend

I make a good Soup!

Says 'POTATO PETE'

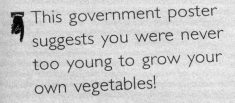

This government poster suggests you were never too young to grow your own vegetables!

DIG FOR VICTORY

DIG FOR VICTORY

There was a special 'Dig for Victory!' song you could sing while you worked, to help keep you cheerful.

Dig! Dig! Dig!
And your muscles will grow big!
Keep on pushing the spade.
Don't mind the worms;
just ignore their squirms.
Dig! Dig! Dig for Victory!

Have you ever done anything for charity? During the war, children took part in lots of different campaigns, all designed to help the war effort. These happened not just at school, but in the evenings, at weekends and during the holidays.

METAL COLLECTORS WANTED
Help collect unwanted metal objects.
Scrap metal can be used to make:
- grenades
- soldiers' helmets
- fighter planes

Children collecting metal for missile production.

The Squander Bug

The government created a cartoon character called the 'Squander Bug'. He was a great big, hairy insect who wanted people to waste money. Instead, both children and adults were encouraged to lend the government money by buying National Savings certificates. The government used this money to help pay for the war. After the war, the money was paid back.

Simple jobs

How could you have helped to win the war? The government produced a leaflet for boys called *Simple jobs boys can do themselves – and so help win the war*. It included instructions on, amongst other things, how to change a fuse and how to clear out a blocked sink.

DON'T TAKE THE SQUANDER BUG WHEN YOU GO SHOPPING

This is the Squander Bug. He has Hitler's symbol on his body to show he's the enemy!

Useful jobs

Could you make a pair of slippers out of a hat to help win the war? Girls were given a leaflet called *Useful jobs girls can do – to help win the war*. As well as making slippers, it taught how to mend a drawer and how to fix a knife handle.

17

Afternoon Post

During World War Two, just about everybody had relatives serving in the **armed forces**. Each day, children would be waiting to hear from their dads or brothers.

A little boy listens as his mother reads a long-awaited letter from his father.

Snail mail

Getting news was difficult during the war. There was no email, no internet and no mobile phones. News had to come by letter. For soldiers, sailors and airmen abroad, this could take weeks, or even months, as their letters had to be sent by ship. Usually, letters were delivered twice a day – once in the morning and once in the afternoon.

Bad news

There was also the kind of news that no family wanted to hear: news that husbands, fathers or brothers had been injured, taken prisoner or killed in action.

War-time telegrams

Important messages about servicemen killed or 'missing in action' were sent by telegram. Telegrams were delivered by a 'telegram boy', usually on a bike. If you saw a telegram boy call at a house, it was likely to be bad news.

Post Office telegram boys ready to be given their telegrams to deliver.

Tuesday 18 February 1941

Just eating tea when Pam Smith burst in waving a **telegram**:

CONFIRM – ABLE SEAMAN LESLIE SMITH ALIVE AND WELL.

Last week, Pam's mum had a telegram saying Leslie (Pam's big brother) had drowned at sea! Seems it was another Leslie Smith who drowned. Later, I caught mum staring into the fire. Knew what she was thinking right enough – hope our dad's safe, too.

Children playing on a bomb site never knew what they might find.

Dangerous play

After bombing raids, many children played in the streets. There were empty, bombed-out houses that were dark, creepy and often very dangerous! Sometimes children accidentally picked up **unexploded bombs**. As most men were at war and most women were at work, there weren't many grown-ups around to watch the children.

War games

Lots of games children played had a war theme. There weren't many toys, so children used their imaginations. Sticks became rifles and old prams became tanks!

Think About It!

ID cards

Imagine always having to carry a special card with your name and address on it. During the war, everyone had to carry an Identity (ID) Card. They were important because, if you got separated from your family during an air raid, rescue workers would know where you lived.

A child's Identity Card. 👈

> **Saturday 8 March 1941**
> Jonny Wilkins came round. Showed me a bit of old metal. Said it's a bit off one of the **incendiary bombs** that landed on Albion Street. Why would I be interested in a bit off one of Hitler's bombs? Honestly! Boys.

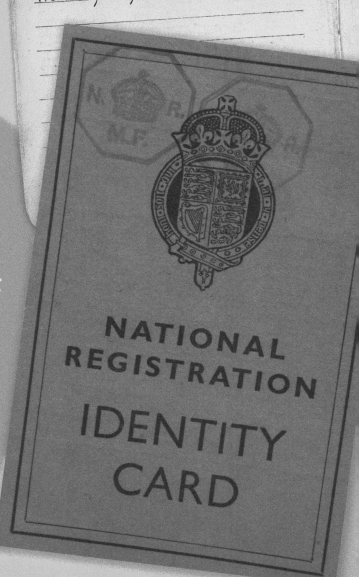

NATIONAL REGISTRATION IDENTITY CARD

N.R. M.F.

What's for Tea?

"What's for tea, Mum?"

The answer would have been, "Not a lot, and not much choice," during the war. Enemy submarines were sinking many of the ships that brought food to Britain from abroad, so lots of food was rationed by the government, including meat, butter, biscuits and worst of all – sweets! The only sort of meat that wasn't rationed was offal – the leftover bits like ox tail. Yummy!

A child's and grown-up's ration books.

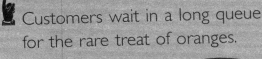
Customers wait in a long queue for the rare treat of oranges.

Do you like eggs?

During the war, even eggs were rationed. People were allowed only one egg every two weeks, so they got used to using powdered eggs. They often used powdered milk, too.

Sunday 16 March 1941
Gran showed me how to make something new for dinner – Lord Woolton Pie. It has lots of vegetables in it but no meat.

It's quite nice really. Even Marjory ate hers without moaning. Tomorrow Gran is going to teach me how to make Beetroot Pudding. Yuk! Sounds revolting!

Think About It!

LORD WOOLTON

Lord Woolton was the Government Minister for Food in the war. The pie was named after him!

The Ministry of Food

Imagine going shopping with your ration book. Everyone had one. Grown-ups had light brown ones; children had blue ones. When you went shopping, the things you bought were crossed off in your ration book by the shopkeeper. The **Ministry of Food** published special recipes to help people make their rations go further.

What do you think we should ask my Gran to cook us for tea? Pizza or Beetroot Pudding?

That should be an easy decision!

Things to Do After Tea

What do you like to do after tea? Watch TV? Go on the internet? Play computer games? Of course, at the time of the war, computers and the internet hadn't yet been invented – and, although the first television broadcasts were made in 1936, very few homes had a TV.

Children from better-off families had toys to play with. Many of these toys had war themes, like toy soldiers and model aircraft.

DID YOU KNOW?

Many cinemas had special Saturday morning children's film clubs. There'd be cartoons and exciting serials, often about heroes like Zorro.

Children would get up on a Saturday to go to the morning film club.

The wireless

Most homes had a radio (or wireless, as they were often called). There was a special programme for children on the BBC called *Children's Hour*. It had stories, plays and talks on subjects such as wildlife and astronomy. Strangely enough, *Children's Hour* was never an hour long – only forty-five minutes!

Of course, you might have found yourself writing a letter to your dad.

A 1940s radio. It is made of Bakelite – an early type of plastic.

Monday 24 March 1941

Dear Dad,
I hope you're well. We have been busy here, collecting for the war effort. Jonny Wilkins took his family's metal bath in for scrap. He said it would be made into a Spitfire, which was better than having a bath every week. I miss you and hope you come home on leave soon. Or better that the war ends and you come back for good.

Lots of love,
Joan xxx

Blackout Time

What colour are the curtains in your bedroom? In World War Two you would most likely have had black or very dark curtains. The reason was that if there was a light showing from your house, it could help guide German pilots towards their targets, such as factories, docks or railway lines – so everyone had to cover their windows with thick, heavy curtains.

A dark world

Outside at night, streetlights were turned off and car headlights had slotted covers fitted over them. This was called the 'blackout'.

Blackout curtains had to block out every bit of light.

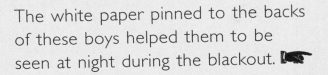
The white paper pinned to the backs of these boys helped them to be seen at night during the blackout.

Tuesday 8 April 1941

On way back from Pam's, I tripped over kerb. Cut my knee! There was blood everywhere! All Hitler's fault! Stupid blackout! When I got in, Mum splashed **iodine** all over it. Mum said I was lucky I didn't walk slap bang into the bus stop and knock myself out.

Think About It!

Air Raid wardens

During a blackout, not a single ray of light was allowed to escape from your house – Air Raid wardens made sure of that. They would stand in the street and shout "Put that light out!" Some people thought they were very bossy, but they had an important job to do.

DID YOU KNOW?

Many people criss-crossed tape over their windows to help prevent glass shattering and causing injuries if a bomb fell.

Taping up all the windows in your house would look really weird!

Time for Bed

Winter evenings can be quite cosy, can't they?
Nice roaring fires or central heating, a warm
duvet to snuggle up into when you go to bed …

Friday 18 April 1941

Bedtime. Kept clothes on. Put dressing
gown over top of clothes. This way:

1. I'm ready to race down to
   the shelter when the air raid
   sirens start
2. I'm not quite so cold.

Marjory's asleep. Snoring. Gave her
my old teddy bear with the missing
eye. Might stop her grizzling in the
shelter. Will stop writing my diary for
now. Got this book Miss Bagthorpe
gave me I want to read. It's called
Little Women. All about four sisters
growing up in America. Will take it
with me down the shelter.

Coal rationing

In World War Two, you
would have found things very
different. There was no central
heating and, if you were poor,
very little coal for the fire. Even
well-off families were short
of coal, because it was … yes,
you've guessed it, rationed. Coal
had to be saved for the factories
and the railways.

Most trains were steam trains
needing coal. Trains ferried
goods, war supplies — and soldiers
— all around the country.

Imagine getting into bed, pulling the covers over you, but all the time wondering how long you'd be there before you heard the air raid siren.

A child's bedroom ... complete with potty under the bed!

Think About It!

Going potty

To avoid having to go outside to the toilet at night, most people had a large china 'potty' under their beds to use instead.

After the War ...

W orld War Two lasted from 1939 to 1945. It is estimated that 60 million people worldwide died in the war. About 40 million were **civilians**, including children.

Victory!

Germany and her European allies surrendered on 8 May 1945. In Britain, this was known as VE (Victory in Europe) Day. Japan didn't surrender until 15 August 1945. This was called VJ (Victory in Japan) Day.

Tuesday 8 May 1945
Had a big VE Day party in our street. Helped Mum make jellies. Marjory was very sick.

Thursday 25 October 1945
Dad came home. Mum,
Marjory, me all in tears.
Baby Alan yelling like mad.
First time he's ever seen
his dad!

DID YOU KNOW?

Gradually rationing ended, but it took a long time. Sweet rationing didn't end until 1953, eight years after the end of the war!

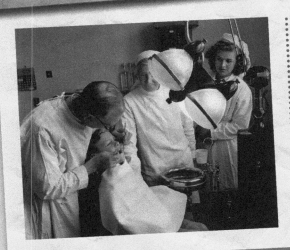

Open Wide!

In Britain a new government was elected that promised a better future for everyone. New homes and schools were built. A National Health Service was created providing free health care – including visits to the dentist.

Glossary and Index

air raid	attack by aircraft dropping bombs
all clear	siren that was sounded once an air raid was over
armed forces	members of the navy, army and air force
Blitz	comes from the German *Blitzkrieg*, which means 'lightning war'. Used to describe bombing attacks by the German air force
Civil Defence	people who helped look after civilians during the war
civilians	people who were not in the armed forces
concentration camps	prison camps set up by Adolf Hitler's government. Few prisoners in these camps survived for more than six months
government propaganda	information put out by the government to persuade people to support the war effort
incendiary bomb	bomb designed to start a fire when it explodes
iodine	antiseptic ointment used for cuts and grazes
Ministry of Food	government department responsible for the supply of food
ration	fix an amount of a particular thing, e.g. petrol, beef, cloth, to make sure there was enough for everyone
refugees	those forced to leave their own country by war or bad treatment
Soviet Union	former group of countries in Eastern Europe and Northern Asia, of which Russia was the largest
telegram	message sent between post offices using telephone wires
unexploded bomb	bomb that hasn't exploded on landing

---

air raid shelters 4, 5, 10
air raid sirens 4, 28, 29
air raid wardens 27
baths and toilets 6, 29
blackout 26–27
bombs 4, 5, 9, 10, 11, 20, 21, 27
cinemas 24
Civil Defence 9
clothes 14
coal 28

evacuees 11
food and meals 2, 12, 15, 22–23
gas masks 7
Identity (ID) Cards 21
Jewish people 3
letters and telegrams 18–19, 25
London 5, 9, 10, 11
'make do and mend' 14, 17
metal collections 16, 25
National Health Service 31

National Savings certificates 17
radios 25
rationing 6, 8, 14, 22, 28, 31
refugees 3
schools 8–9, 10, 11, 12–15
songs 13, 15
toys and games 13, 21, 24
vegetable growing 12, 15
war effort 14, 16–17, 20, 25
World War Two 2–3, 30